D0931791

TERRORS FROM THE DEEP

TRUE STORIES OF SURVIVING SHARK ATTACKS

by Nel Yomtov

illustrated by
Narciso Espiritu

Haverstraw King's Daughters
Public Library
10 West Ramapo Road
Garnerville, NY 10923

GRAPHIC LIBRARY™

CAPSTONE PRESS
a capstone imprint

Graphic Library is published by Capstone Press,
1710 Roe Crest Drive, North Mankato, Minnesota 56003
www.capstonepub.com

Copyright © 2016 by Capstone Press, a Capstone imprint.
All rights reserved. No part of this publication may be
reproduced in whole or in part, or stored in a retrieval system,
or transmitted in any form or by any means, electronic,
mechanical, photocopying, recording, or otherwise, without
written permission of the publisher.

Library of Congress Cataloging-in-Publication Data
Cataloging-in-publication information is on file with the
Library of Congress.
ISBN 978-1-4914-6573-8 (library binding)
ISBN 978-1-4914-6577-6 (eBook PDF)

Editorial Credits:
Anthony Wacholtz, editor; Ashlee Suker, designer;
Nathan Gassman, creative director; Laura Manthe,
production specialist

Editor's note:
Direct quotations, noted in purple type, appear on the
following pages:

Page 3, chapter 1: Michael Capuzzo. *Close to Shore: The
Terrifying Shark Attacks of 1916*. New York: Crown, 2003,
p. 103.

Page 3, chapter 3: https://www.youtube.com/
watch?v=lSsZr1agCyY, 2:05.

Page 3, chapter 5: http://www.washingtonpost.com/wp-dyn/
content/article/2009/07/14/AR2009071403248.html

Page 4, headline 1: http://www.newser.com/story/193443/
great-white-attacks-2-kayakers-off-mass-coast.html

Page 4, headline 2: http://www.newser.com/story/178411/
teen-killed-by-shark-while-body-boarding.html

Page 4, headline 3: http://www.newser.com/story/171911/2-
shark-attacks-close-hawaii-beaches.html

Page 8: *Close to Shore: The Terrifying Shark Attacks of 1916*,
p. 103.

Page 14: http://www.thesurfchannel.com/news/travel/
20131007/dual-14ft-shark-attack-victim-the-story-
of-shannon-ainslie/

Page 16: Bethany Hamilton. *Soul Surfer*. New York: Gallery
Books, 2004, p. 71.

Page 20: http://www.wkrg.com/story/23151864/shark-attack-
victim-recounts-terrifying-ordeal

Page 25: http://sharkattacksurvivors.com/shark_attack/
viewtopic.php?f=39&t=899

Printed in the United States of America
in North Mankato, Minnesota.
042015   008823CGF15

TABLE OF CONTENTS

SHARK ATTACK!

GREAT WHITE ATTACKS 2 KAYAKERS OFF MASS. COAST

TEEN KILLED BY SHARK WHILE BODY-BOARDING

SHARK ATTACKS CLOSE 2 HAWAII BEACHES

These astonishing 2013 and 2014 headlines gripped public attention around the world. For most people, the words "shark attack" stir up feelings of terror and panic. We often describe sharks as fierce, bloodthirsty, and savage. Yet statistics show that sharks should fear us. On average, sharks kill five to 10 humans each year. On the other hand, humans kill anywhere from 20 to 100 million sharks annually in commercial and sport fishing.

Both hunter and hunted, sharks emerged as the rulers of the oceans as long as 420 million years ago. They live in all of the world's oceans, and several species can be found in both seawater and freshwater.

Sharks vary in size and length. The dwarf lantern shark has a maximum length of about 8 inches (20 centimeters). On the other hand, the harmless whale shark can reach lengths of 46 feet (14 meters).

Today nearly 500 species of shark prowl the oceans. Among these, great white, bull, and tiger sharks account for most of the attacks on humans. Sharks of each of these deadly species bare their teeth in the following true stories. Bold, quick-thinking people used their wits and courage to overcome incredible danger. Their stories demonstrate the power of their will to survive.

CHAPTER ONE

JOEY DUNN "IT WAS GOING TO SWALLOW ME!"

In the first week of July 1916, sharks attacked and killed two swimmers on the New Jersey coast. On July 12, Joseph "Joey" Dunn, his brother, Michael, and a friend raced to Matawan Creek for a refreshing swim. Fourteen-year-old Joey had no idea these cool waters, 11 miles (18 kilometers) inland from the ocean, held the nightmare of a lifetime.

The boys began swimming in the late afternoon, when the tide was going out.

Hey, Mike! Hey, Jerry! I bet I can swim to the other side of the creek before you!

Bet you can't, little brother! Jerry and I are the best swimmers in town!

Minutes later, a man from town came running to the creek.

Hey, you kids! Get out of the water! There's been a shark attack upstream! Get out!

C'mon, Joey! Swim to the dock as fast as you can!

W—wait for me, Mike!

The older, stronger boys reached the dock first.

C'mon, Joey! Swim faster!

As Joey swam, something big and rough scraped against his body.

Mike! Something touched me!

Then he felt a tug at his leg that threatened to pull him underwater.

Help me, Mike!

Hang on, Joey!

UNNH! UNNH!

Hurry! It's pulling him under!

Joey later recalled, "It seemed the fish was trying to get my whole leg inside his mouth ... I thought it was going to swallow me."

Jacob Lefferts, who had been issuing shark warnings from his motorboat, witnessed the attack.

Help! Help!

A shark has that kid!

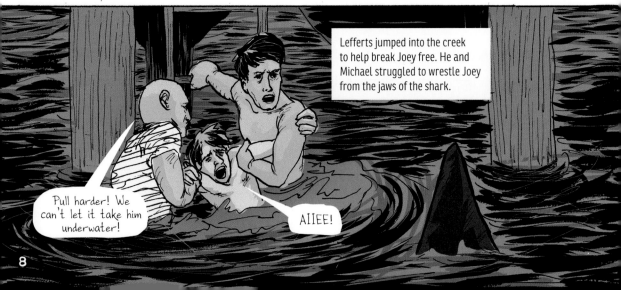

Lefferts jumped into the creek to help break Joey free. He and Michael struggled to wrestle Joey from the jaws of the shark.

Pull harder! We can't let it take him underwater!

AIIEE!

8

Joey and his rescuers reached the dock ladder. As Joey pulled himself up, the shark took another bite on his leg.

AAAH!

Mike and Lefferts finally pulled Joey free of the shark's grip. Joey was raced to a nearby hospital.

Easy, Joey. I promise you'll be okay.

Unhhh …

Doctors treated Joey's badly torn leg, and he was able to recover.

Of the five victims of the 1916 New Jersey attacks, Joey Dunn was the lone survivor. Two days after his attack, hunters caught a great white shark near Matawan Creek. Human flesh and bones were found in the shark's belly. Many people believe it was the same shark that attacked Joey and killed two other people that day.

CHAPTER TWO

RODNEY FOX WHEN COURAGE TRIUMPHS

On December 8, 1963, Rodney Fox participated in a spearfishing contest at Aldinga Bay, South Australia. The 23-year-old was the region's current champion, and he was eager to keep his title. Fox was about a half mile (0.8 km) from shore when he spotted a large butterfish and dived after it. As he prepared to fire his speargun at his prey, Fox felt a powerful thump on his chest. From that moment on, Fox's life would never be the same.

A great white shark had grabbed Fox firmly in its huge jaws. Fox gouged at the shark's eyes, hoping it would release him from its death grip.

It's working! I feel him letting go!

When Fox pushed the great white, his arm plunged deep into the creature's mouth. As he pulled out his arm, the shark's razor-sharp teeth sliced his hand and arm to the bone.

Fox swam toward the surface with the shark in pursuit. The creature grabbed the fish float and fish line clipped to his belt.

He'll pull me down if I don't get free of this float and line!

The great white dragged Fox deeper and deeper into the sea.

C-can't breathe!

Just as Fox was about to open his mouth and breathe in water ...

SCHLIK!

It bit through the line! I've got to get to the surface before it attacks again!

When Fox reached the surface, two friends pulled him aboard a small motorboat.

I – I can't believe I made it.

Hang on, mate. We'll get you to shore in a flash.

The shark had ripped open a lung, crushed Fox's ribs, and mangled his right hand. It took more than 450 stitches to put the fisherman back together.

I'm one lucky Australian!

Since the attack, Fox has devoted his life to studying and protecting great white sharks.

CHAPTER THREE

SHANNON AINSLIE "I THOUGHT I WAS GOING TO DIE"

On July 17, 2000, 15-year-old Shannon Ainslie and several friends were surfing the rolling waves of Nahoon Reef near East London, South Africa. As he rode a wave, Shannon had no idea he was about to become the victim of one of the strangest and most terrifying shark attacks on record.

Looking good, little brother!

Shannon's really charging that wave!

As Shannon surfed, a great white shark rammed his board from underneath.

KRUNCCH!

The impact sent the helpless surfer hurtling into the air before plunging back into the water.

Noooo!

The shark grabbed Shannon's right hand in its massive jaws. It dragged him backward and deeper under the water.

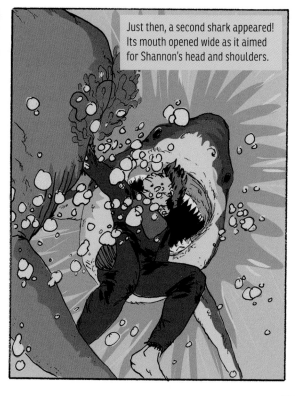

Just then, a second shark appeared! Its mouth opened wide as it aimed for Shannon's head and shoulders.

With both sharks in striking distance, Shannon flailed helplessly in the water. He later recalled, "This all happened so quickly that I had no clue what was going on."

FWAPPP!

The collision knocked Shannon free of the first shark's jaws. For several moments, the hunter and the hunted stared at each other face to face. Would the beast attack again?

Luck was on Shannon's side. The great white slowly swam past him and then disappeared into the water.

I've got to get back to shore!

Shannon swam to the surface and saw his surfboard floating between him and the beach. He hopped on and paddled toward shore.

My fingers are nearly torn off!

After several minutes, Shannon neared the shore.

Call the ambulance!

Get him onto shore!

It took 30 stitches to repair the damage. Two of his fingers had to be sewn back onto his hand.

But Shannon was back in the water six weeks later—not far from where he had been attacked.

CHAPTER FOUR

BETHANY HAMILTON BRAVE SURFER

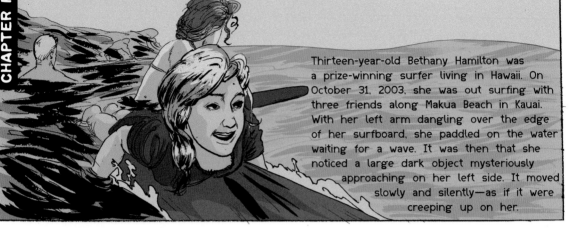

Thirteen-year-old Bethany Hamilton was a prize-winning surfer living in Hawaii. On October 31, 2003, she was out surfing with three friends along Makua Beach in Kauai. With her left arm dangling over the edge of her surfboard, she paddled on the water waiting for a wave. It was then that she noticed a large dark object mysteriously approaching on her left side. It moved slowly and silently—as if it were creeping up on her.

In an instant, a 14-foot (4.3-m) tiger shark attacked Bethany. She later recalled, "It was over in a few seconds. ... Then I saw that my arm had been bitten off almost to the shoulder."

Badly bleeding—and 20 minutes from shore—the young surfer was now in a race for her life. She began paddling to shore with one arm. Her dad, Holt, swam to her while giving instructions to his son, Byron.

I'll push you from behind, Beth! Get to the beach as fast as you can, Byron! Call for help!

Holt pushed Bethany by the tail of her surfboard until they reached a reef.

I'll tie my rash guard around you tight. It will stop the bleeding.

Please, God, let me get back to the beach.

Holt paddled toward shore for 15 minutes.

Bethany, are you still with me?

I'm okay, I'm okay.

Hang on, Beth. We'll be there soon.

Byron reached the beach first. He used a cell phone to call for help.

Be strong, Beth. You're doing fine.

The shark had bitten off Bethany's left arm above the elbow. She had lost more than 60 percent of her blood and was in shock.

Bethany was rushed to the hospital, where she spent a week in recovery. Just three weeks after the attack, she was back surfing the waters around Hawaii.

The tiger shark that attacked Bethany was caught and killed 1 mile (1.6 km) from the attack site. It still had pieces of Bethany's surfboard in its mouth.

CHAPTER FIVE

CHUCK ANDERSON "THEY'RE VICIOUS AND THEY'RE MEAN"

On June 9, 2000, Chuck Anderson was swimming off Gulf Shores, Alabama, in the Gulf of Mexico. About 100 yards (91 m) offshore, he felt something ram him from below. Although the 44-year-old swimmer didn't see what struck him, he knew exactly what it was.

As Anderson treaded water, he put his face down in the sea to locate his attacker.

Where did he go?

In a flash, the shark came up from the bottom. Anderson tried to push it away, but the beast bit into his hand and took off four fingers in one swift snap.

Ee-agghh!

SHOMP

Anderson's attacker—an 8-foot (2.4-m), 325-pound (147-kilogram) bull shark—slowly swam away. As blood poured from Anderson's hand, he once again searched for his foe.

The shark returned a third time and sunk its teeth into Anderson's stomach.

Then the beast circled away yet again.

When the shark returned a fourth time, Anderson tried to push it off. The creature pounced on his arm.

Ugghh!

The shark sped toward the bottom of the gulf, dragging Anderson down with him. Later recalling the terrifying event, Anderson said "the shark slung me around like I was a rag doll."

I'm going to die...

People on the beach who saw the attack said Anderson was underwater for about two minutes.

Then the shark surged back to the surface. Trying to push himself away, Anderson slammed his free hand against the beast's nose.

FWAP

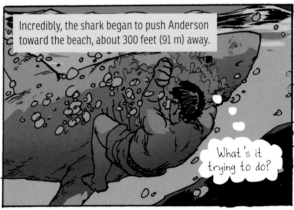

Incredibly, the shark began to push Anderson toward the beach, about 300 feet (91 m) away.

What's it trying to do?

They both ended up on a sandbar in shallow water. Anderson tried to wriggle free.

I can't hold out much longer!

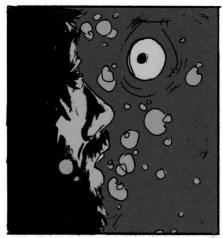

Anderson wriggled his arm up and down and finally jerked it out hard. His hand had been bitten off and his arm was torn to the bone.

Eee-aggh!

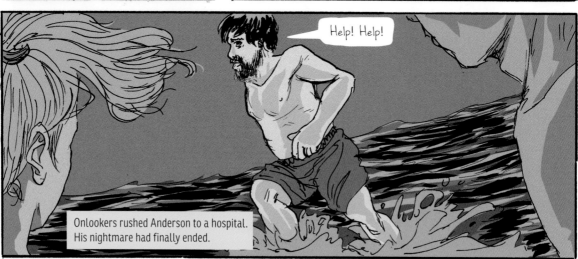

Help! Help!

Onlookers rushed Anderson to a hospital. His nightmare had finally ended.

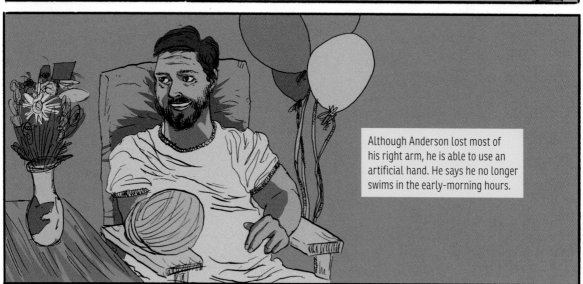

Although Anderson lost most of his right arm, he is able to use an artificial hand. He says he no longer swims in the early-morning hours.

CHAPTER SIX

ERIC NERHUS INTO THE SHARK'S MOUTH

On January 23, 2007, Eric Nerhus was searching for abalone, a prized shellfish, off the southeast coast of Australia. At a depth of about 30 feet (9 m), Nerhus pried shellfish from the ocean bed with a chisel. His son, Mark, was in a fishing boat at the water's surface above.

Nerhus never saw his attacker race toward him through the cloudy waters.

The 10-foot (3-m) great white shark snapped its massive jaws around Nerhus' head. The impact crushed the diver's facemask into his nose.

Nerhus also lost his air tube, which was connected by a hose to an air tank in the fishing boat above.

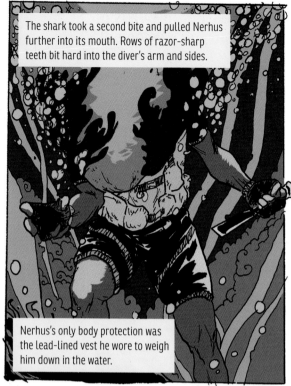

The shark took a second bite and pulled Nerhus further into its mouth. Rows of razor-sharp teeth bit hard into the diver's arm and sides.

Nerhus's only body protection was the lead-lined vest he wore to weigh him down in the water.

As the great white shook Nerhus from side to side, the diver desperately tried to think of an escape.

I've got to force it to release me!

Nerhus frantically jabbed at the shark's eye with his chisel.

I'm a dead man if this doesn't work!

The shark reacted by opening its mouth just enough for Nerhus to wriggle out.

No air. Can't breathe.

Nerhus estimated that he was in the shark's mouth for about two minutes without his air supply.

Nerhus managed to put the air tube back in his mouth. But he was still in big trouble.

Will it attack again?

I have to hurry!

As Nerhus swam to the surface, the shark circled around his flippers.

24

Nerhus narrowly missed having his legs bitten off.

Mark! There's a shark, there's a shark! Get me to shore!

Nerhus was put onto a speedboat, which took him on an hour-long trip to shore.

Hang in there, Eric. We'll get to a hospital soon.

I've never experienced anything like the fear I felt inside those jaws.

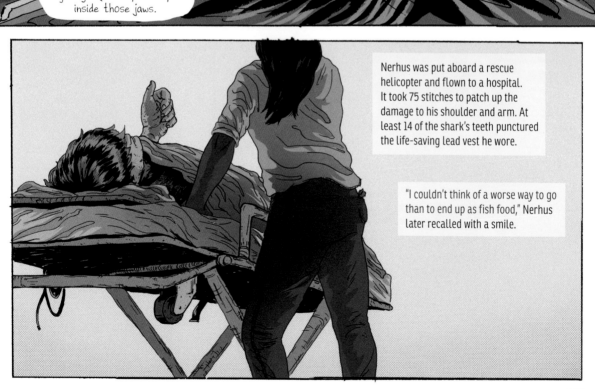

Nerhus was put aboard a rescue helicopter and flown to a hospital. It took 75 stitches to patch up the damage to his shoulder and arm. At least 14 of the shark's teeth punctured the life-saving lead vest he wore.

"I couldn't think of a worse way to go than to end up as fish food," Nerhus later recalled with a smile.

CHAPTER SEVEN

TODD ENDRIS SAVED BY DOLPHINS

On August 28, 2007, 24-year-old Todd Endris was enjoying a late-summer day of surfing at Monterey Bay in California. As he waited for a perfect wave, a pod of dolphins splashed playfully a short distance away. Because dolphins were a common sight, Endris paid little attention to them. Several minutes later, however, he would be grateful for their presence.

As Endris kept an eye out for a good wave, a 13-foot (4-m) great white shark violently struck his board from below. The impact sent the surfer flying 15 feet (4.6 m) into the air.

Whooaa!

Endris landed in the water headfirst. The great white attacked again, this time chomping down on Endris' torso. The shark had Endris and the surfboard in its monstrous jaws!

Hunff! Hunff!

Endris fought for his life, punching at the shark's eyes. For a moment, the shark released him.

Then it attacked again, trying to swallow Endris' right leg. The surfer kicked the great white in the head and snout again and again.

I can't keep this up much longer!

The shark released Endris. As the great white was about to move in for the kill, the pod of dolphins swam to the scene.

Can they really be coming to rescue me?

The dolphins thrashed the water with their tails and made high-pitched sounds.

EEEE!

SPLATT!

EEEE!

SPLATT!

Endris' rescuers swam underneath him and between him and the shark.

SPLATT!

SPLATT!

EEEE!

It's working! The shark is turning away!

EEEE!

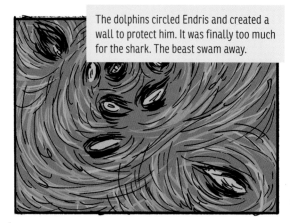

The dolphins circled Endris and created a wall to protect him. It was finally too much for the shark. The beast swam away.

I can't believe what just happened!

Get on your board and paddle!

Slow down your breathing so you don't lose any more blood.

Todd and his friend caught a wave and reached the beach. A group of friends gathered to help the injured surfer.

Endris was rushed to a hospital on a helicopter. He had lost 50 percent of his blood. It took 500 stitches to repair the damage to his torso and leg.

Six weeks later, Todd Endris returned to surf at the exact spot where he was attacked.

Haverstraw King's Daughters
Public Library
10 West Ramapo Road
Garnerville, NY 10923

GLOSSARY

ABALONE *(ab-uh-LOH-nee)*—a large sea snail with a flat shell

COMMERCIAL *(kuh-MUHR-shuhl)*—to do with buying and selling things

GOUGE *(GOUJ)*—to cut deeply

POD *(POD)*—a group of certain kinds of sea animals, such as dolphins or whales

PREY *(PRAY)*—an animal hunted by another animal for food

PUNCTURE *(PUHNGK-chur)*—to make a hole with a sharp object

PURSUIT *(pur-SOOT)*—the act of trying to catch someone or something

REEF *(REEF)*—a strip of sand, rock, or coral close to the surface of the ocean

SPEARFISHING *(SPEER-fish-ing)*—catching fish with a weapon with a long handle and a pointed head

SPECIES *(SPEE-sheez)*—a group of plants or animals that share common characteristics

TREAD *(TRED)*—to stay upright in the water by using your arms and legs

READ MORE

Leavitt, Amie Jane. *A Daredevil's Guide to Swimming with Sharks.* North Mankato, Minn.: Capstone Press, 2013.

MacQuitty, Miranda. *Shark.* New York: DK Publishing, 2014.

Owings, Lisa. *Bull Shark Attack.* Minneapolis: Bellwether Media, 2013.

Tarshis, Lauren. *I Survived the Shark Attacks of 1916.* New York: Scholastic, 2010.

INTERNET SITES

FactHound offers a safe, fun way to find Internet sites related to this book. All of the sites on FactHound have been researched by our staff.

Here's all you do:

Visit *www.facthound.com*

Type in this code: 9781491465738

Check out projects, games and lots more at
www.capstonekids.com

INDEX